P9-DHA-553

GOD'S GIFT

Retold by Jean Richards   Illustrated and Designed by Norman Gorbaty

A Doubleday Book for Young Readers

A Doubleday Book for Young Readers

Published by
Delacorte Press
Bantam Doubleday Dell Publishing Group, Inc.
1540 Broadway
New York, New York 10036

Doubleday and the portrayal of an anchor with a dolphin are trademarks of
Bantam Doubleday Dell Publishing Group, Inc.

Copyright © 1993 by Chardiet Unlimited, Inc.
Illustrations copyright © 1993 by Norman Gorbaty
Published by arrangement with Chardiet Unlimited, Inc.
All rights reserved. No part of this book may be reproduced or transmitted
in any form or by any means, electronic or mechanical, including photocopying,
recording, or by any information storage and retrieval system, without the
written permission of the Publisher, except where permitted by law.

Library of Congress Cataloging in Publication Data

Richards, Jean Hosking.
God's gift / Retold by Jean Richards; illustrated by Norman Gorbaty.
   p.   cm.
Summary: A simple retelling of the story from Genesis of how
God created the first man and then made creatures, including
the first woman, to keep him company.
ISBN 0-385-31092-7
Bible stories, English — O.T. Genesis.   2. Creation — Juvenile literature.
[1. Bible stories — O.T. Genesis.   2. Creation.]
I. Gorbaty, Norman, ill.   II. Title.
BS652.R49   1993
222′.1109505 — dc20   92-38265   CIP   AC

Manufactured in Mexico

October 1993

10 9 8 7 6 5 4 3 2 1

The illustrations for this book were stenciled
on illustration board with printing ink.
The book is set in 18 point Times Roman.
The design is by Norman Gorbaty.

For Tally, my gift
J.R.

For Joy,
and the animals –
Lisa, Bill,
Ben, Andrea,
Becky and Lizzie
N.G.

In the beginning
God made the earth and the sky,
and when He was done,
He sat down to rest.
He could hear the singing of the wind
and the roar of the sea.
God was glad.

But after a while He noticed
that He was all alone in this great,
vast, empty world.
God thought: Wouldn't it be nice
to share this beautiful creation?

As He was thinking this,
some water gurgled up from
deep inside the earth.
It made the earth into a soft clay.
God decided to make something.
He put His hands
into the warm clay
and formed Man.

God was happy
because now Man would
keep Him company
in this great,
vast, empty world.
But Man was not
good company.
Man didn't talk or play
or dance or sing.
He just stood there
like a lump of clay,
which was, of course,
exactly what he was.

Then God had an idea.

"I will blow the breath of life into Man."

He got very close to Man's face and blew hard.

Some of God's breath went through Man's nose and mouth, deep down into him.

Suddenly one of Man's arms moved.

And then his hand.

And then his fingers.

Man took a step.

And then another.

Man looked up at God and smiled.

Man liked being alive.

God wanted Man to have
a nice place to live,
so He planted
a beautiful garden.
In this garden were lovely trees
full of delicious fruits and nuts.
Then God placed Man in the garden
to watch over it
and enjoy it.

For a while Man was happy,
but then he began to feel lonely.
God decided that Man
should have someone to keep him company.
"I will make many new creatures,"
God said to Man, "and you
must give each of them a name.
Then you will choose the
one you want for your partner."

Then God put His hands
into the mushy clay again
and made a huge body
with four thick legs
and a thin tail
To this he added a big head
with *floppy ears and a lo-o-o-o-o-o-o-o-o-o-o-o-ong nose.*

God set it down next to Man.
"How wonderful!" said Man.
"I think I shall call it Elephant."
"Elephant," repeated God.
"A fine name
for a creature so big."
Elephant
flapped its ears
and lumbered off
into the garden.

Then God

scooped up another glob of clay.

He rolled four strong legs and a body.

He added a big head with a thick mane

and then a long, thin tail

with a tiny tuft on the end.

"How grand!" exclaimed Man.

"I will call it Lion!"

"Lion it is!" agreed God.

Lion proudly swished its tail

and padded off into the garden.

God could hardly wait to work on His next creation.

This time He rolled a lump of clay until

and the other end the tail.

it got so long He couldn't hold it any longer. One end was the head,

It was very slithery. "Snake," said Man. "I shall definitely call it Snake."

And Snake flicked its tongue and wiggled off into the garden.

God thought
He would make
something different.
He took a pinch of clay
and made a tiny body
with a tiny head and
six miniature legs.

Then He added two wings.
God thought that the
wings looked too plain,
so He painted them
with bright colors.

He placed it in the air,
and the creature
began to flap its wings.
"How exquisite!" said Man.
"I think I shall name it
Butterdog."

But God frowned.
Man thought and thought.
Maybe Butterdog was
not the right name.
"I have it!" he cried.
"Butterfly!"

The minute Man
said the word,
Butterfly took off
gracefully
into the sky.

God continued making creatures, some large, some small, some round, some tall. Finally He asked Man, "Which of these creatures will be your partner?"

"They're all splendid creatures," said Man sadly, "but not one of them is right for me. I want someone who is almost like me but just different enough."

Then God
made Man fall
into a deep sleep.
He took a bone
from his side
and added clay to it
until He had made something
that looked almost like Man
but was different.
Then He blew
the breath of life into it.

When Man woke up,
he saw the creature.
Never before had Man
seen something so lovely.
For a long time Man couldn't
say anything.
Finally he said to her,

"I
shall
call
you
Woman."

When Woman heard Man,
she did not rush off into the garden.
She stayed right where she was
and looked at Man and smiled.

God looked down at Man
and Woman and all the creatures
He had made, and He was pleased.
The world was still great and still vast...

...but not so empty anymore.

And that is the old, old story of how the first man and the first woman and all the other creatures came to be.